GUMBO'S ON THE MENU

Cooking with Serenity: Gumbo's on the Menu!

Publisher: Black Moms Reality Bookcase LLC™, Suffolk, Virginia (USA)

Trim Size: 8.5" × 8.5" • **Format:** Full color • Hardback & Paperback • **Page Count:** 52

ISBNs: Hardback 978-1-956911-36-7 • Paperback 978-1-956911-34-3 • eBook (optional)

Library of Congress Control Number: Not available at the time of printing.

BISAC: JNF / Cooking & Food • Holidays / General • People & Places / African American & Black

Keywords: kids cookbook, cooking for kids, New Orleans recipes, gumbo, family cooking, classroom cooking

Distribution: Ingram (iPage) • Direct Publisher • eBook via OverDrive/Libby (optional)

Library/Wholesale Terms: 35% discount • Returnable • PO accepted • Net 30

Standards: SOL/SEL alignment available • Educator guide included

Author: Michelle Knight

This is a work of fiction for educational and entertainment purposes. Names, characters, places, and incidents are imaginative or used fictitiously. Always supervise children during cooking activities.

Printed in the United States of America • 10 9 8 7 6 5 4 3 2 1

Contact: blackmomsrealitybookcase@gmail.com • 225-333-7070 • BMRBookcase.com

Dedication

To the heart and soul of New Orleans—

This book is dedicated to the resilient spirit of our beloved city. Through hurricanes like Katrina and even the shadow of terrorist attacks, we have stood strong—rebuilding, healing, and uniting with the same passion that seasons every pot of gumbo and fills every kitchen with love.

There is no place in the world like New Orleans. Our culture runs deep, our music never stops, and our food—our food tells stories of strength, family, and celebration.

To every dad who learned to stir the pot standing beside their own father, this book is for you. And to every child who now pulls up a chair to learn the same—it's your turn. May these pages remind you that no matter what we face, we come back to the table, stronger and full of flavor.

With love,
Author Michelle Knight

Author Michelle Knight

Serenity woke up early Saturday morning, bright-eyed and bushy-tailed, excited for the day.

"It's Gumbo Day!" she yelled.

Serenity always looked forward to cooking with her dad, but today's meal would be special. Today, they would cook a New Orleans favorite, which was also Serenity's favorite. Their family would join them for dinner that evening, so it had to be right!

Serenity ran into her parents' room and hopped on their bed like a frog jumping onto a lily pad.

"Get up, Daddy! It's Gumbo Day! Get up!" Serenity shouted, unable to control her excitement.

"Okay," Mr. Wilton said while laughing.

"Hurry, Daddy! We must get started."

"Yes, princess," Mr. Wilton replied as Serenity dashed out of the room to get dressed.

Whenever she and her dad cooked, Serenity wore her favorite dress and an apron with the words "Daddy's Little Chef" on the front. Instead of a chef's hat on her head, she wore a shiny crown her mom gave her on her 8th birthday. It made her feel like the queen of cooking.

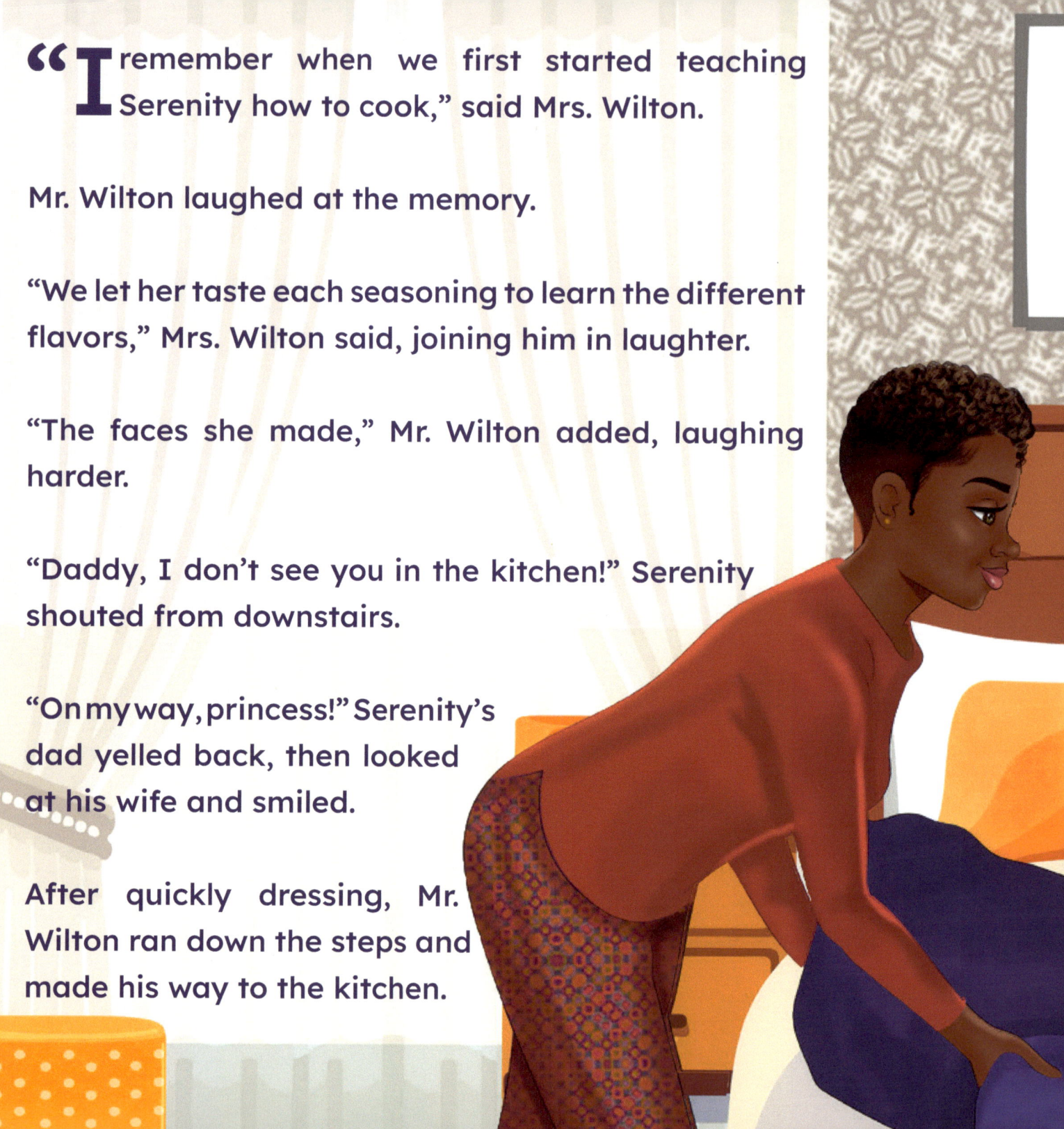

"I remember when we first started teaching Serenity how to cook," said Mrs. Wilton.

Mr. Wilton laughed at the memory.

"We let her taste each seasoning to learn the different flavors," Mrs. Wilton said, joining him in laughter.

"The faces she made," Mr. Wilton added, laughing harder.

"Daddy, I don't see you in the kitchen!" Serenity shouted from downstairs.

"On my way, princess!" Serenity's dad yelled back, then looked at his wife and smiled.

After quickly dressing, Mr. Wilton ran down the steps and made his way to the kitchen.

"I grabbed everything for the gumbo out of the fridge except for the eggs, Daddy. I made a checklist, too," Serenity told him.

"Ummm, princess, why do you have the hot dogs and bologna out? We're not making your grandma's gumbo," Mr. Wilton said, chuckling.

"Ooooooh, I'm going to tell mawmaw what you said!" Serenity replied with a serious face.

"Okay, okay. Sorry," Mr. Wilton said, smirking. "But we won't need those items, princess," he told her.

After putting the items back in the fridge, Serenity turned and asked, "Daddy, can I cut up some of the veggies?"

"Yes, but only using a butter knife," responded Mr. Wilton.

"But, Daddy, I told all my friends I was cooking like a real chef today," Serenity whined, pouting.

"Who's going to know? Daddy is just trying to protect the cook's cute little fingers," he chuckled and gave her stomach a tickle.

Serenity laughed at his playfulness.

Then, while pretending to be in front of a television audience for a cooking show, Mr. Wilton smiled and announced, "Today, we will be making a delicious seafood gumbo. My assistant will be none other than the lovely Princess Serenity."

Serenity smiled so brightly that she lit up the kitchen like a ray of sunshine.

"Before we start, let's make sure we have all of our ingredients," Serenity's father said. "You check them off as I call them out. Okay, Assistant Chef?" yelled Mr. Wilton.

"Yes, Chef!" Serenity replied while hopping up and down like a rabbit from joy.

"Wait!" Serenity suddenly shouted. "Chefs cannot work without an apron," she told her dad before grabbing his apron hanging on a hook in the kitchen.

"Thank you. Now, let's get to work," Mr. Wilton said after tying on his apron.

About to burst from joy, Serenity smiled from ear to ear.

"Ready for the ingredients, Assistant Chef Serenity?" he asked.

"Yes, Chef," Serenity answered.

"Cooking oil!" Mr. Wilton called out.

"Check, Chef!" Serenity yelled back.

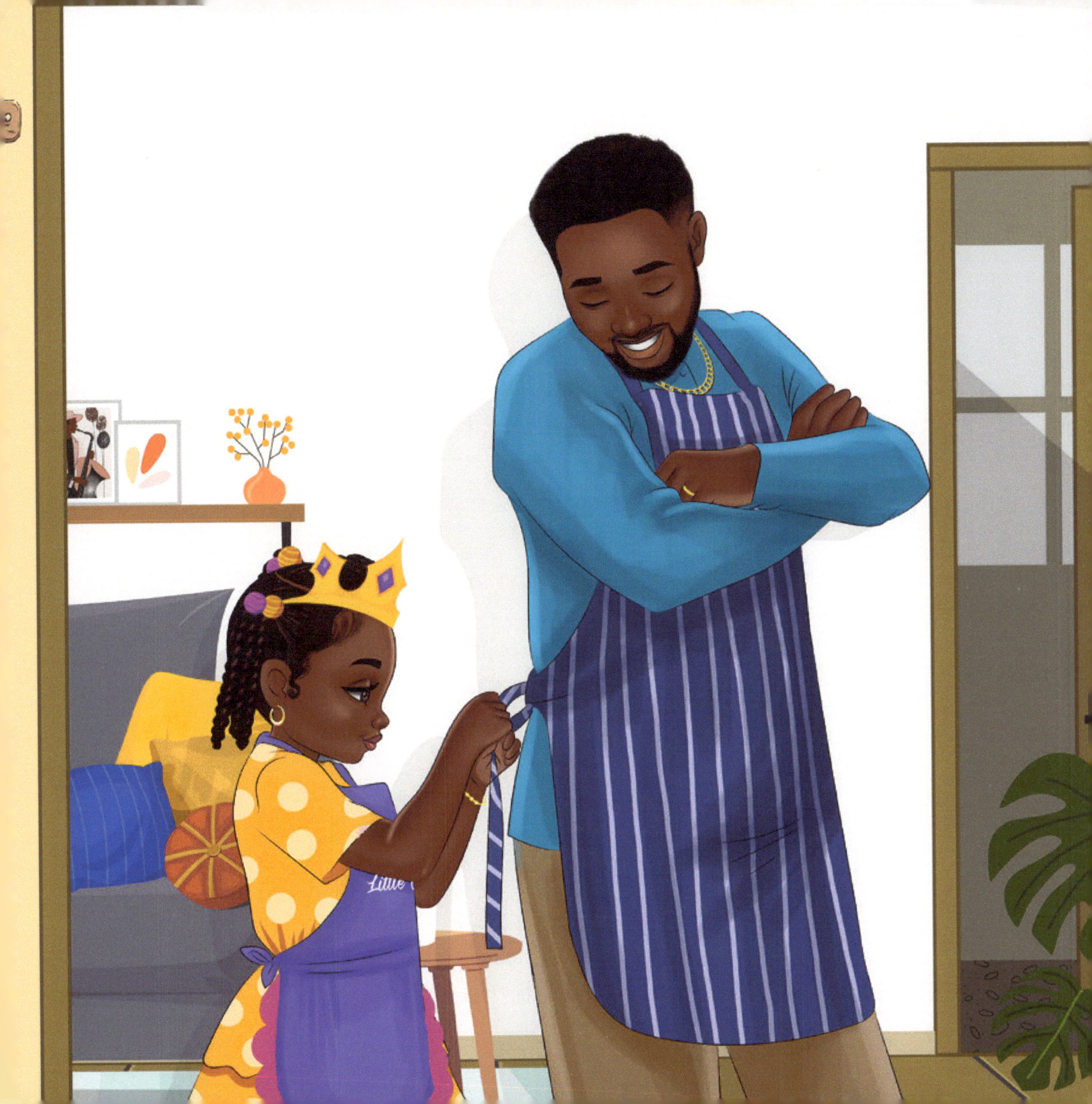
Little

With each ingredient Mr. Wilton called out, Serenity grew increasingly excited. She was more than ready to start cooking.

"Flour!", "Green, yellow, and orange bell peppers!", "Onions!", "Celery!"

The list grew longer than Serenity's arm as her dad continued calling out the ingredients.

"Garlic!", "Shrimp!", "Turkey sausage!", "Chicken broth!"

When Mr. Wilton noticed Serenity standing there with an awkward look on her face, he asked, "Are you keeping up, princess?"

"This sure is a lot of ingredients for one pot. Will they all fit?" Serenity asked, looking puzzled.

Mr. Wilton laughed. "We'll have more than enough room for the pot we will use."

By the time Mr. Wilton finished naming all the ingredients, Serenity was lying on the floor wearing a sad expression.

"Is it time to cook yet?" Serenity asked.

"Almost, princess. First, we must cut up some of the ingredients. You cut the bell peppers, and I will roll the hot sausage."

"Daddy, can we just drop everything in the pot the way it is?" Serenity whined.

Smiling, Mr. Wilton replied, "This will be quick. I promise."

"Okay, everything is cut and rolled," Mr. Wilton announced. "You're an awesome assistant," he said, complimenting Serenity. Serenity beamed with pride.

"Now, the most im-portant part of making gumbo is your roux," Mr. Wilton said, using a serious tone.

"What's a roux, Daddy?" Serenity asked. "Sounds like voodoo."

Mr. Wilton laughed so hard and loud that tears rolled down his face. Mrs. Wilton ran into the kitchen to see what had happened.

"Mom, Daddy is talking about voodoo!" shouted Serenity, sounding scared.

"What?" Mrs. Wilton said, looking at her husband.

"Serenity and I are about to make the roux for the gumbo," explained Mr. Wilton.

Serenity's mother started laughing. Serenity couldn't figure out what was so funny.

"It's not voodoo, sweetheart. Roux is the seasoning mixture created with love that makes the gumbo so special," Mrs. Wilton told her.

oil

"**A**re you sure Daddy is not doing voodoo?" cried Serenity.

"Yes, I'm sure," Mrs. Wilton said, giving Serenity a huge momma bear hug.

"Come on, sweetie. We have work to do," Serenity's dad told her.

"We sure do, Chef! I hope your heart is ready to put your love in our gumbo!" Serenity replied, now smiling again. Then she leaned over to her dad and whispered, "Please leave enough love in your heart for me and Mom."

"Absolutely," Mr. Wilton whispered back.

Once they finished cutting up the ingredients, Serenity patiently watched her dad create the roux for the gumbo. She was amazed at how everything was coming together. The aroma made their house smell like a restaurant. Serenity's mouth began to water, and her stomach growled.

"Is it ready yet?" asked Serenity while doing her bathroom dance.

"No, sweetheart. Not yet," Mr. Wilton replied, chuckling at his daughter's excitement to taste the dish.

Serenity asked every ten minutes if the gumbo was finished as she imagined the delicious flavors in her mouth. She tried playing with her dolls, doing flips around the house, and watching her favorite TV show, but time was moving as slow as a turtle.

Family members finally began to arrive, ringing the doorbell and coming inside to get settled.

"Yay! The gumbo must be ready!" Serenity shouted while jumping up and down.

"**J**ust a little longer, sweetheart," Mr. Wilton told her. "I'm adding the finishing touches."

Serenity stepped back and let out a huge sigh.

"Serenity, when you want something done right, you must have patience with the process. Do you understand, sweetheart?"

"Yes, Chef," Serenity replied, then walked off to join her family in the living room.

She wished the gumbo was ready to eat.

After what felt like forever, her dad yelled, "Serenity, it's ready!"

Serenity could have jumped to the moon!

"**D**ad, can I have the first bowl of gumbo?" she asked.

"Of course," Mr. Wilton replied.

"And Mom has to get the second bowl so we can be the first ones to eat a bowl of your love," Serenity said with a smile as she went to sit at the table.

Gumbo Day turned out to be the best day for Assistant Chef Serenity. It was worth the wait.

GUMBO ESSENTIALS:
Where Flavor Begins

No conversation about gumbo can begin without honoring its soul—the Holy Trinity. In Cajun and Creole kitchens, this sacred blend of onion, bell pepper, and celery is the very foundation of flavor.

The Holy Trinity

Onions:
Yellow, white, or sweet onions all work beautifully.

Bell Peppers:
Green is the classic choice, but red, yellow, or orange can be used for a sweeter, more colorful variation.

Celery:
Include the leafy tops—they carry just as much flavor as the stalks.

A Balanced Blend

Traditionally, the Holy Trinity is used in equal parts (1:1:1). This balance creates a depth of flavor unique to Southern cuisine.

A Nod to the French

The Holy Trinity is Louisiana's answer to the French mirepoix (onion, celery, and carrot). Instead of carrots, we use bell peppers- bringing a Southern boldness to a classic technique.

Flavor with Soul

This aromatic base isn't just about taste—it's about tradition. It's the first thing in the pot and the last thing you forget. Some chefs add garlic to the mix too, affectionately calling it "The Holy Trinity with the Pope."

RESPECT THE ROUX

If the Trinity is the soul, then the roux is the spirit. It thickens, deepens, and elevates the gumbo into something unforgettable.

Patience Is Key:

A rushed roux is a ruined roux. Cook it low and slow, stirring constantly, until it turns the color of milk chocolate—rich, nutty, and deeply flavorful.

Baking Method (Yes, Really!):

For a hands-off option, some cooks bake the roux in the oven. It takes longer, but requires less babysitting.

Whether stirred on the stove or slowly baked, the roux is worth every second.

Cooking with Serenity means cooking with love, patience, and intention. Now that you know the secrets—go make your gumbo with confidence, and don't forget to stir with your heart.

GUMBO RECIPE

From Cooking with Serenity: Gumbo's on the Menu

⏱ Prep Time: 30 min   ⏱ Cook Time: 1 hr 30 min   Servings: 8–16 (Makes 16 cups)

Ingredients

For the Gumbo:

- 1 medium green bell pepper, diced (1½ cups)
- 1 medium yellow onion, diced (1¾ cups)
- 3 celery stalks, diced (1½ cups)
- 6 garlic cloves, minced
- ½ bunch fresh parsley, coarsely chopped (optional, ½ cup)
- 2 to 3 tablespoons salt-free Cajun seasoning, divided (see Notes)
- 2 teaspoons dried thyme
- 2 bay leaves
- ½ teaspoon cayenne pepper (adjust to taste)
- 1 pound boneless, skinless chicken thighs, or 1 rotisserie chicken
- 1½ teaspoons kosher salt (plus more as needed)
- 1½ teaspoons freshly ground black pepper
- 14 ounces andouille sausage, sliced into ½-inch rounds
- ½ cup plus 1 tablespoon neutral cooking oil (such as canola or vegetable), divided
- 6 cups low-sodium chicken broth, room temperature
- 2 teaspoons filé powder (optional)
- ½ cup all-purpose flour

Equipment

- Cutting board & knife
- Measuring cups & spoons
- Medium & small bowls
- Large pot or Dutch oven
- Wooden spoon

LET'S COOK!

Always wash your hands first!

1. Prep the Veggies

Dice the bell pepper, onion, and celery; place them in a medium bowl. Mince garlic and chop parsley (if using); place in a small bowl with 2 tbsp Cajun seasoning, black pepper, thyme, bay leaves, and cayenne. Stir to combine..

2. Prepare the Chicken

If using raw chicken, dice into 1-inch pieces and season with salt, pepper, and 1 tbsp Cajun seasoning. If using rotisserie chicken, shred about 4 cups and discard the skin and bones—no additional seasoning needed.

3. Brown the Sausage

In a large pot or Dutch oven over medium-high heat, cook the sausage rounds until browned and fat is rendered (about 5 minutes). Remove and set aside.

4. Brown the Chicken

Add 1 tbsp oil to the same pot. Cook raw chicken until browned, about 10 minutes. Transfer to the plate with sausage.

Skip this step if using rotisserie chicken. Alternatively, you can boil chicken thighs for 30 minutes instead of browning

LET'S COOK!

5. Make the Roux

Combine ½ cup flour and ½ cup oil in the pot. Stir constantly over medium heat until the roux turns a deep milk chocolate color (10–20 minutes). It will go from floury to toasty to nutty—don't walk away! Burnt roux means starting over.

6. Build the Base

Add the Holy Trinity mixture to the roux, stirring to coat. Cook for 10 minutes until onions are translucent. Add garlic mixture, then return sausage and chicken to the pot with any juices. Cook 2–3 minutes until garlic is fragrant.

7. Simmer

Pour in chicken broth and 6 cups of water. Bring to a boil, then reduce heat and simmer uncovered for 35–45 minutes, until thickened and flavors meld.

Optional Toppings & Sides:

- Thinly sliced scallions
- Cooked white rice for serving

RECIPE NOTES

Cajun Seasoning
If using salted Cajun seasoning, reduce added salt. To make your own: Mix 1½ tsp paprika, 1½ tsp garlic powder, ¾ tsp black pepper, ¾ tsp onion powder, ¾ tsp dried oregano, ¾ tsp dried thyme.

Filé Powder
A natural thickener made from sassafras leaves. Adds earthy, tea-like flavor. Optional but traditional.

Shrimp Version
Use 1 lb peeled, deveined shrimp in place of chicken and sausage. Add during the last 10 minutes. If using alongside, reduce shrimp to 8 oz.

Blue Crabs
The cleaned blue crabs are cleaned, broken in half, and added to the gumbo pot, often towards the end of the cooking process, to ensure they don't overcook.

Tomatoes
To add a Creole twist, purée 1 (14 oz) can of fire-roasted diced tomatoes and add when sausage and chicken return to the pot.

Okra
For a classic thickener and Southern touch, add 8 oz of okra (cut cross-wise into ¼-inch rounds) when adding garlic mixture.

Make Ahead
Gumbo tastes even better the next day! Cool, cover, and refrigerate for up to 2 days. Reheat gently over low heat.

Storage
Store leftovers in airtight containers in the refrigerator for up to 5 days.